The Most Famous Pirates

BY CINDY JENSON-ELLIOTT

Reading Consultant:
Barbara J. Fox
Reading Specialist
Professor Emerita
North Carolina State University

CAPSTONE PRESS
a capstone imprint

Blazers is published by Capstone Press,
1710 Roe Crest Drive, North Mankato, Minnesota 56003.
www.capstonepub.com

Library of Congress Cataloging-in-Publication Data
Jenson-Elliott, Cynthia L.
    The most famous pirates / by Cindy Jenson-Elliott.
    p. cm.—(Blazers)
    Includes bibliographical references and index.
    Summary: "Describes the lives and activities of a variety of famous pirates from
the Golden Age of Piracy"—Provided by publisher.
    ISBN 978-1-4296-8609-9 (library binding)
    ISBN 97891-62065-202-2 (ebook PDF)
    1. Pirates—Juvenile literature. I. Title.
G535.J45 2013
910.4'5—dc23   2011048910

Editorial Credits

Aaron Sautter, editor; Veronica Correia, designer; Marcie Spence, media researcher;
    Laura Manthe production specialist

Photo Credits

Alamy: Everett Collection, Inc., 16, Felix Zaska, 25, InterFoto, 27, Lebrecht Music and Arts
Photo Library, 23, Mary Evans Picture Library, 8, 15; Bridgeman Art Library: International, 7,
19, Look and Learn, 5, Peter Newark Historical Pictures, cover; Capstone, 28; Getty Images:
Leemange, 20; iStockphoto: duncan1890, 11, 12; Shutterstock: Eky Studio, design element

Capstone Press would like to thank Alex Diaz at the St. Augustine Pirate and Treasure Museum
for his help in creating this book.

Printed in the United States of America in Stevens Point, Wisconsin.
032012   006678WZF12

Table of Contents

Piracy Through the Ages

It is the year 1710. A ship suddenly appears flying a black flag with a skull on it. It's a pirate ship! Pirates have **raided** ships and towns for thousands of years. Some pirates became famous for their crimes.

raid—a sudden, surprise attack

Fact

Pirates often did not attack ships that came from their own countries.

Chapter One

Pirates of the 1500s

THE BARBAROSSA BROTHERS

Many people feared the Barbarossa brothers in the early 1500s. These **privateers** sailed on the Mediterranean Sea. They attacked cities and ships for the Ottoman Empire.

privateer—a pirate who is licensed by a country to attack and steal from ships from an enemy country

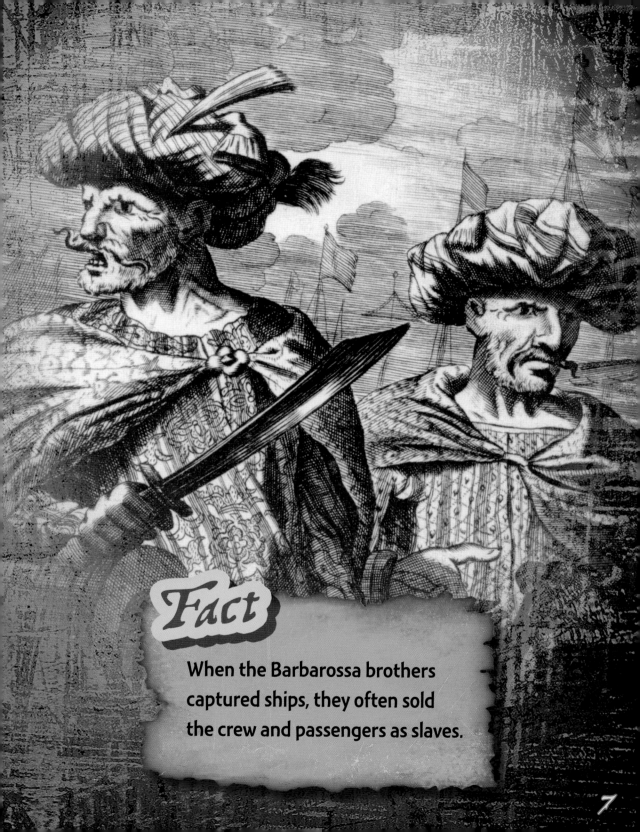

Fact

When the Barbarossa brothers captured ships, they often sold the crew and passengers as slaves.

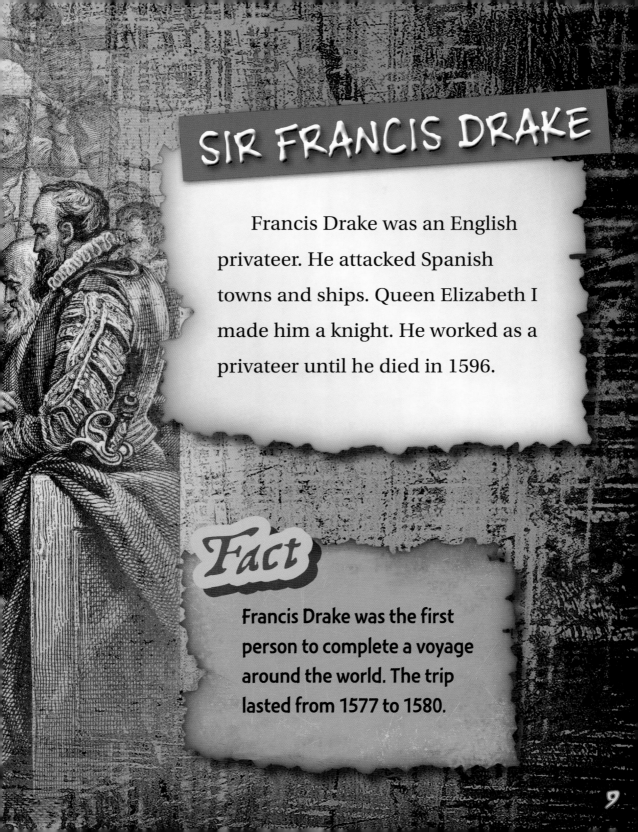

SIR FRANCIS DRAKE

Francis Drake was an English privateer. He attacked Spanish towns and ships. Queen Elizabeth I made him a knight. He worked as a privateer until he died in 1596.

Fact

Francis Drake was the first person to complete a voyage around the world. The trip lasted from 1577 to 1580.

Chapter Two

Pirates of the 1600s

BRETHREN OF THE COAST

In the mid-1600s the Brethren of the Coast worked together in the Caribbean Sea. These **buccaneers** held the first pirate **councils**. The councils created rules that gave pirates rights and made sure they were treated fairly on pirate ships.

buccaneer—a pirate in the Caribbean Sea in the 1600s

council—a group of people who make decisions for a

Fact

The name "buccaneer" came from a wooden frame called a *boucan*. Buccaneer pirates sometimes used boucans for smoking meat.

HENRY MORGAN

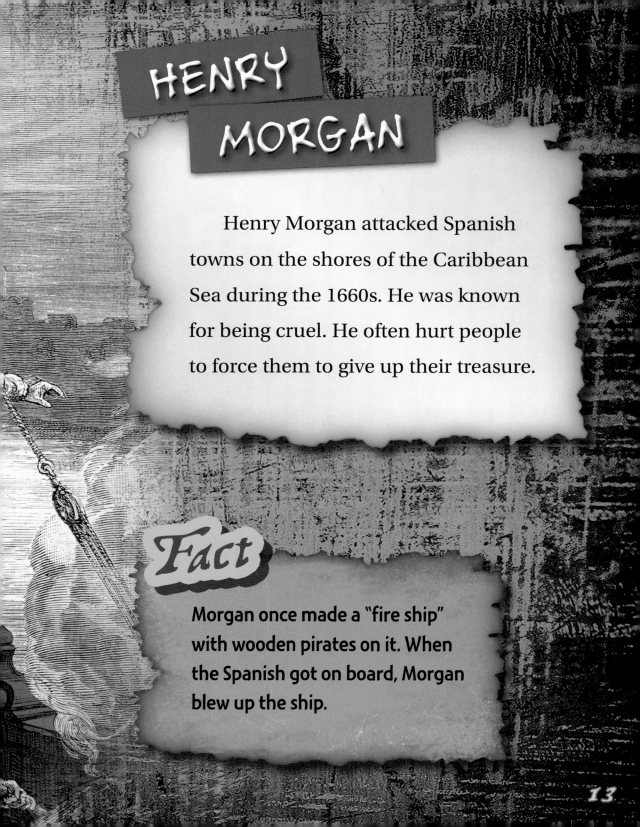

HENRY MORGAN

Henry Morgan attacked Spanish towns on the shores of the Caribbean Sea during the 1660s. He was known for being cruel. He often hurt people to force them to give up their treasure.

Fact

Morgan once made a "fire ship" with wooden pirates on it. When the Spanish got on board, Morgan blew up the ship.

Chapter Three

Piracy's Golden Age (1690-1730)

CAPTAIN WILLIAM KIDD

Captain Kidd set sail as a privateer in 1696. Several rich **investors** paid for his trip. But he kept their money and attacked any ships he chose. Captain Kidd was arrested in 1699. He was hanged for his crimes in 1701.

investor—someone who provides money for a project in return for a share of the profits

Captain Kidd's first ship was called the *Adventure Galley*. After the ship's hull became rotten and leaky, he captured a new ship. He named it the *Adventure Prize*.

HENRY EVERY

Henry Every sailed as a pirate for only about two years. In 1695 he captured a treasure ship from India. The treasure was worth almost 600,000 British **pounds**. Henry Every became the richest pirate in the world in just one daring raid!

Fact

Henry Every disappeared soon after capturing the Indian treasure ship. Some believe he changed his name and went to Ireland in 1696.

pound—a unit of money used in England

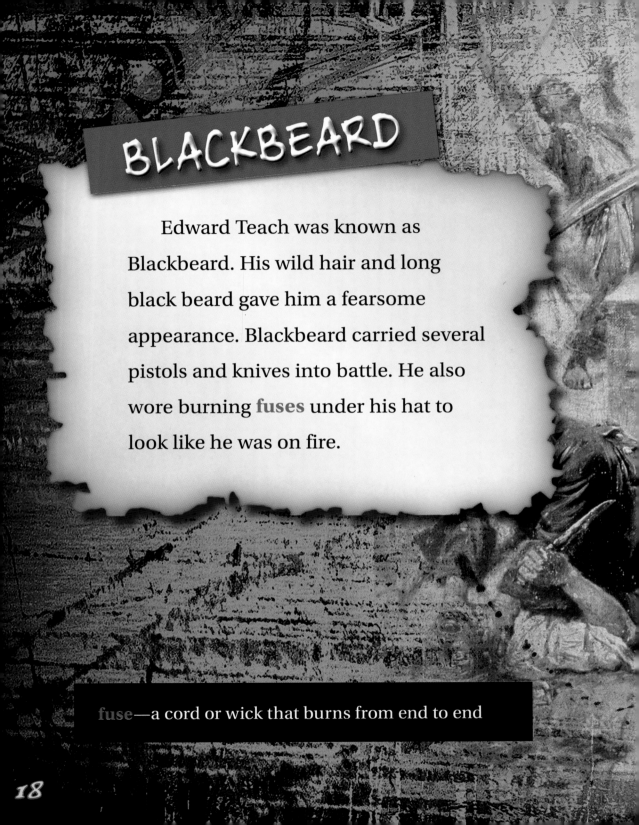

BLACKBEARD

Edward Teach was known as Blackbeard. His wild hair and long black beard gave him a fearsome appearance. Blackbeard carried several pistols and knives into battle. He also wore burning **fuses** under his hat to look like he was on fire.

fuse—a cord or wick that burns from end to end

Fact

Blackbeard was killed in
a fierce battle in 1718. It
took 25 sword wounds and
five gunshots to kill him.

STEDE BONNET

Stede Bonnet was often called "the gentleman pirate." Bonnet was a rich landowner who decided to become a pirate. But he didn't steal a ship. Instead, he paid for his own ship, the *Revenge*. He also paid his crew with his own money.

Fact

Bonnet sailed with Blackbeard for a few months. But Blackbeard later took Bonnet's ship for himself.

BLACK BART

Bartholomew "Black Bart" Roberts was one of the most successful pirates of the Golden Age. He captured more than 400 ships. Black Bart was killed during a battle near the coast of Africa in 1722.

Fact

Black Bart was a fancy dresser. During his last battle, he wore a red suit, a jewel necklace, and a red feather in his hat.

23

Chapter Four

Women Pirates

GRACE O'MALLEY

Most pirates through history were men. But a few women also lived as pirates. Grace O'Malley was a well-known pirate from Ireland. She led attacks against Spanish and British ships in the late 1500s.

STATUE OF GRACE O'MALLEY IN WESTPORT, IRELAND

Fact

Grace O'Malley was a wealthy landowner. She owned at least five castles and the surrounding lands.

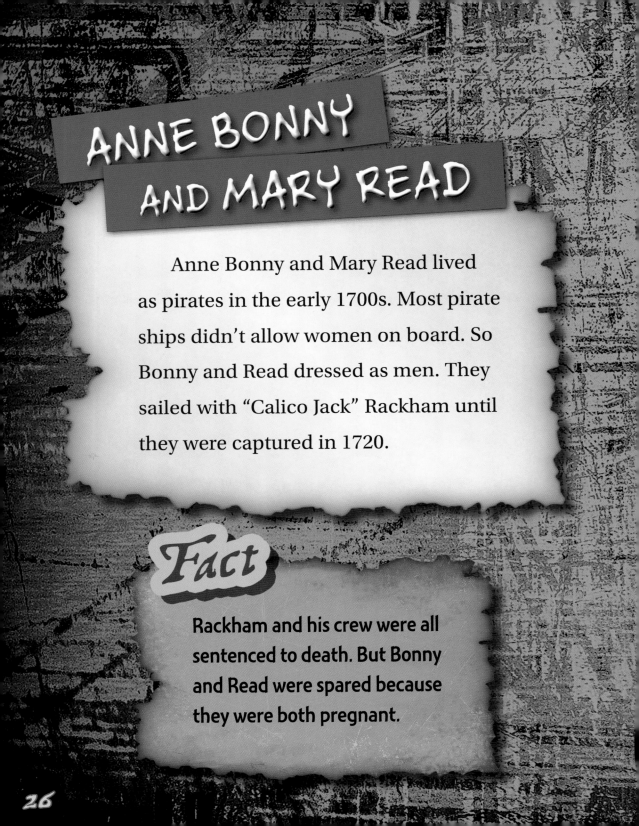

ANNE BONNY AND MARY READ

Anne Bonny and Mary Read lived as pirates in the early 1700s. Most pirate ships didn't allow women on board. So Bonny and Read dressed as men. They sailed with "Calico Jack" Rackham until they were captured in 1720.

Fact

Rackham and his crew were all sentenced to death. But Bonny and Read were spared because they were both pregnant.

ANNE BONNY

MARY READ

27

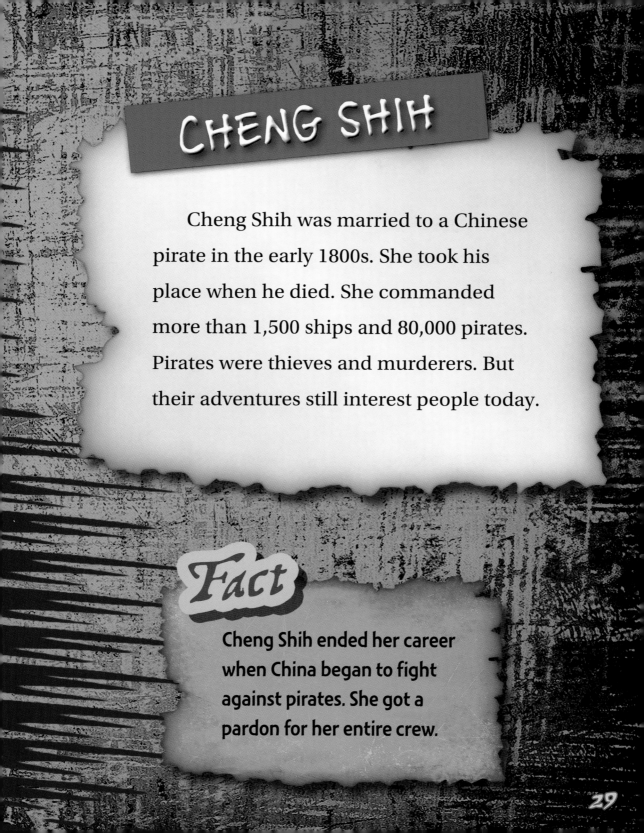

CHENG SHIH

Cheng Shih was married to a Chinese pirate in the early 1800s. She took his place when he died. She commanded more than 1,500 ships and 80,000 pirates. Pirates were thieves and murderers. But their adventures still interest people today.

Fact

Cheng Shih ended her career when China began to fight against pirates. She got a pardon for her entire crew.

Glossary

buccaneer (buh-kuh-NEER)—a pirate in the Caribbean Sea who attacked Spanish ships in the 1600s

council (KOUN-suhl)—a group of people who make decisions for a larger group

fuse (FYOOZ)—a cord or wick that burns from end to end

investor (in-VEST-uhr)—someone who provides money for a project in return for a share in the profits

pardon (PAHR-duhn)—an act of official forgiveness for a serious offense

pound (POUND)—a unit of money used in England

privateer (prye-vuh-TEER)—a pirate who is licensed by a country to attack and steal from ships from an enemy country

raid (RAYD)—a sudden, surprise attack

Read More

Jenson-Elliott, Cindy. *Pirate Ships Ahoy!* Pirates! Mankato, Minn.: Capstone Press, 2013.

Malam, John. *Blackbeard and the Pirates of the Caribbean.* Pirates. Laguna Hills, Calif.: QEB Pub., 2008.

Matthews, John. *Pirates Most Wanted: Thirteen of the Most Bloodthirsty Pirates Ever to Sail the High Seas.* New York: Atheneum Books for Young Readers, 2007.

Internet Sites

FactHound offers a safe, fun way to find Internet sites related to this book. All of the sites on FactHound have been researched by our staff.

Here's all you do:

Visit *www.facthound.com*

Type in this code: 9781429686099

Super-cool stuff!

Check out projects, games and lots more at
www.capstonekids.com

Index